WHAT HAPPENS WI

I go to the DENTIST

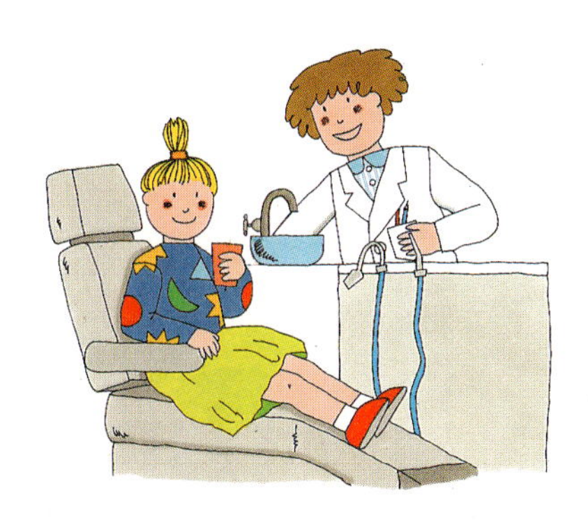

Written by Helen Slater
Illustrated by Lyn Mitchell

Here is Sue and Sue's mum. Mummy has a big friendly grin. But Sue just smiles, because one of her teeth hurts today.

Sue and her friend Ann are walking home from school. Sue is chewing sweets. 'Ouch!' says Sue. 'My tooth hurts.'

That night, Mummy asks Sue, 'Did you brush your teeth?' Naughty Sue tells a lie and says 'Yes, mum!'

A special nurse comes to school the next day. She looks at all the children's teeth, to see if they are healthy. She gives Sue a letter to take home!

'It says that you must go to the dentist to have a filling,' Mummy says. 'Will it hurt?' asks Sue. 'Only a little,' says Mummy.

Sue and her mum go to the dentist's surgery.
'This is where the dentist works,' says Mummy.

Mummy tells the receptionist that Sue has come to see the dentist. 'Please go into the waiting room,' says the receptionist.

Sue reads a comic in the waiting room. 'I'll wait for you in here while you see the dentist,' says Mummy.

'Hello,' says the dentist. 'My name is Mr Watkins. Come in and sit on the chair.'

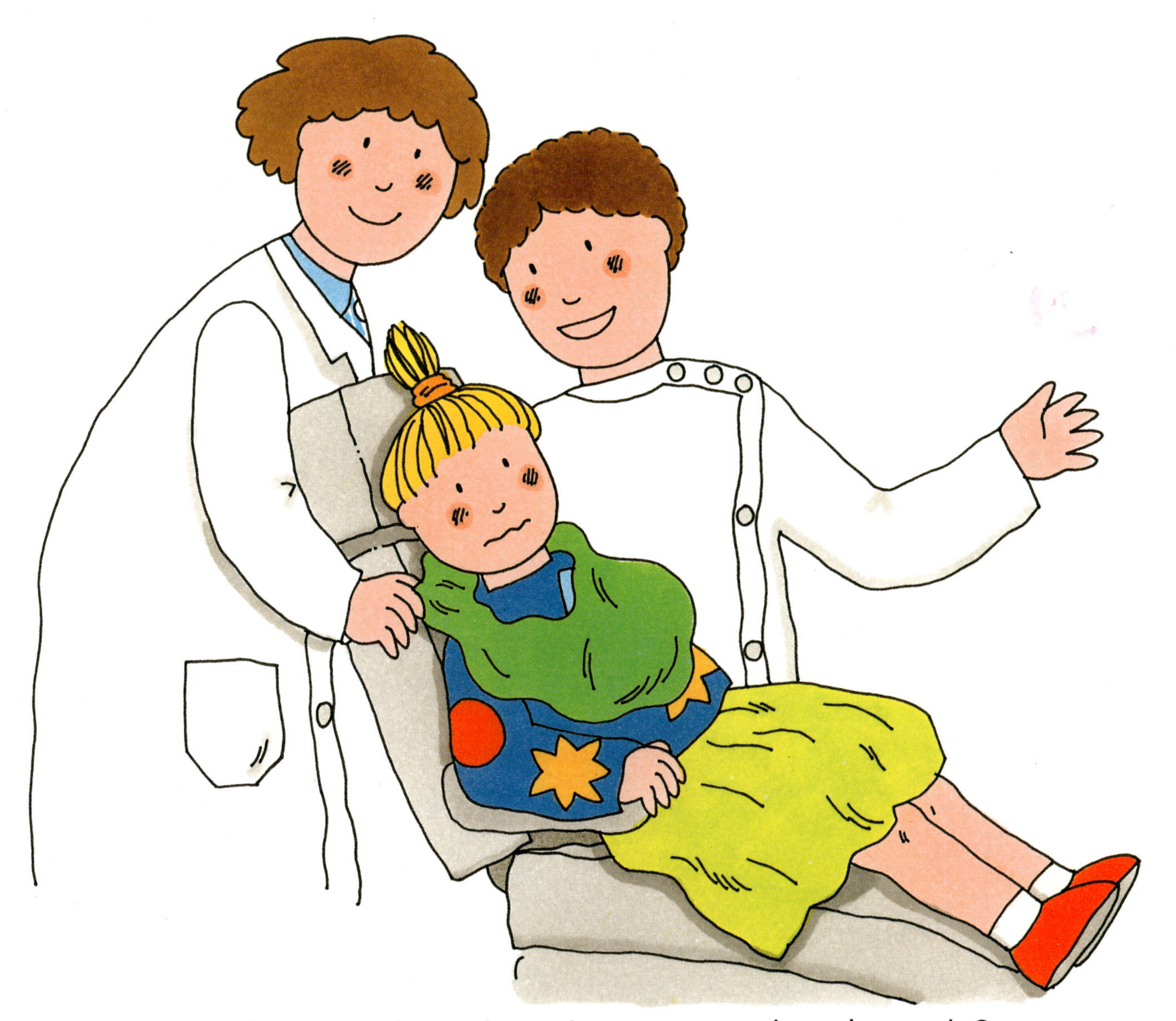

Mr Watkins makes the chair move back until Sue is almost lying down. 'Now I can see inside your mouth easily,' he explains.

'This little round mirror helps me see the teeth right at the back of your mouth,' the dentist tells Sue.

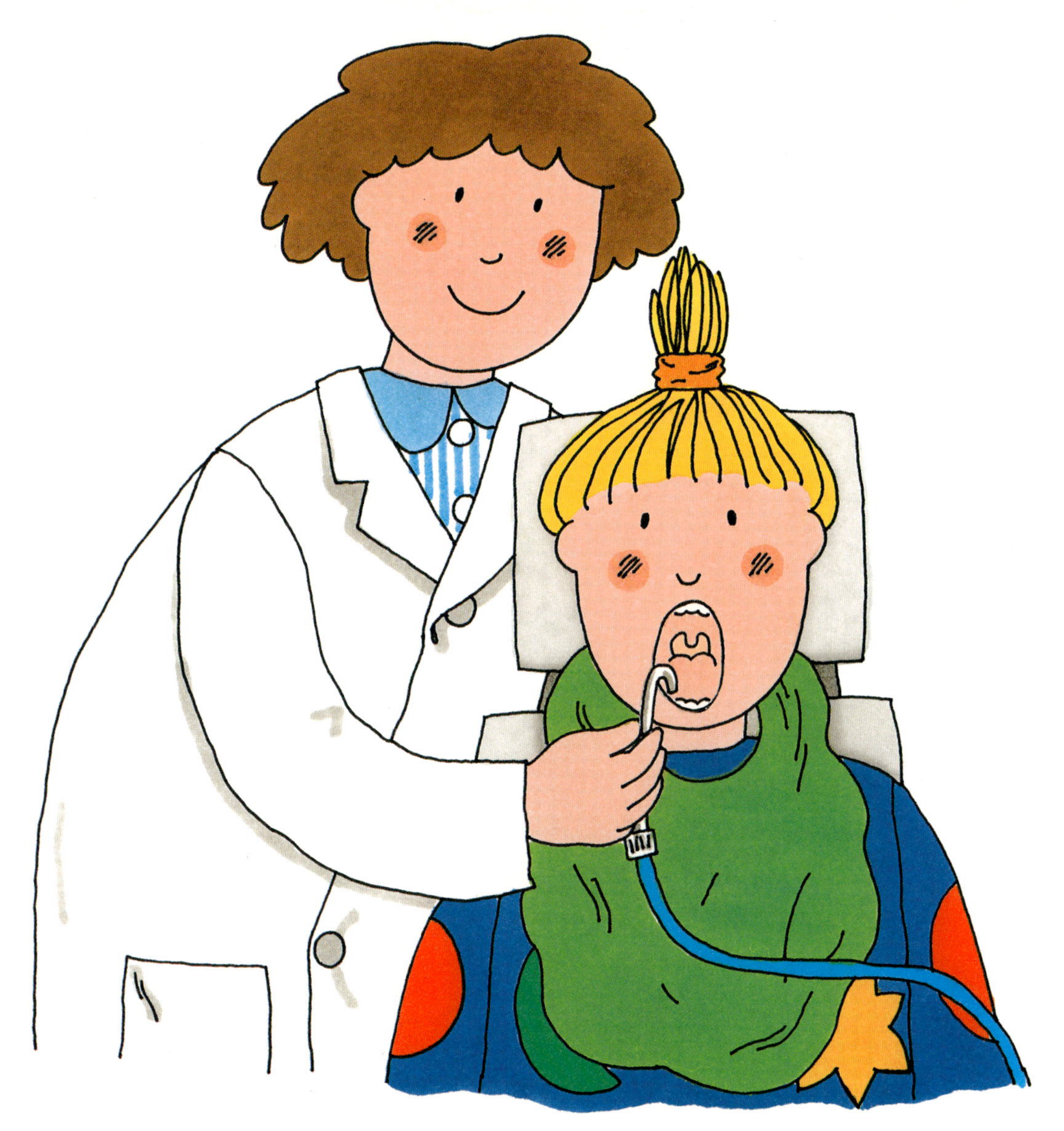

‘Now we will put this little tube inside your mouth,’ says the nurse. ‘It sucks the water out of your mouth so that you won’t have to swallow.’

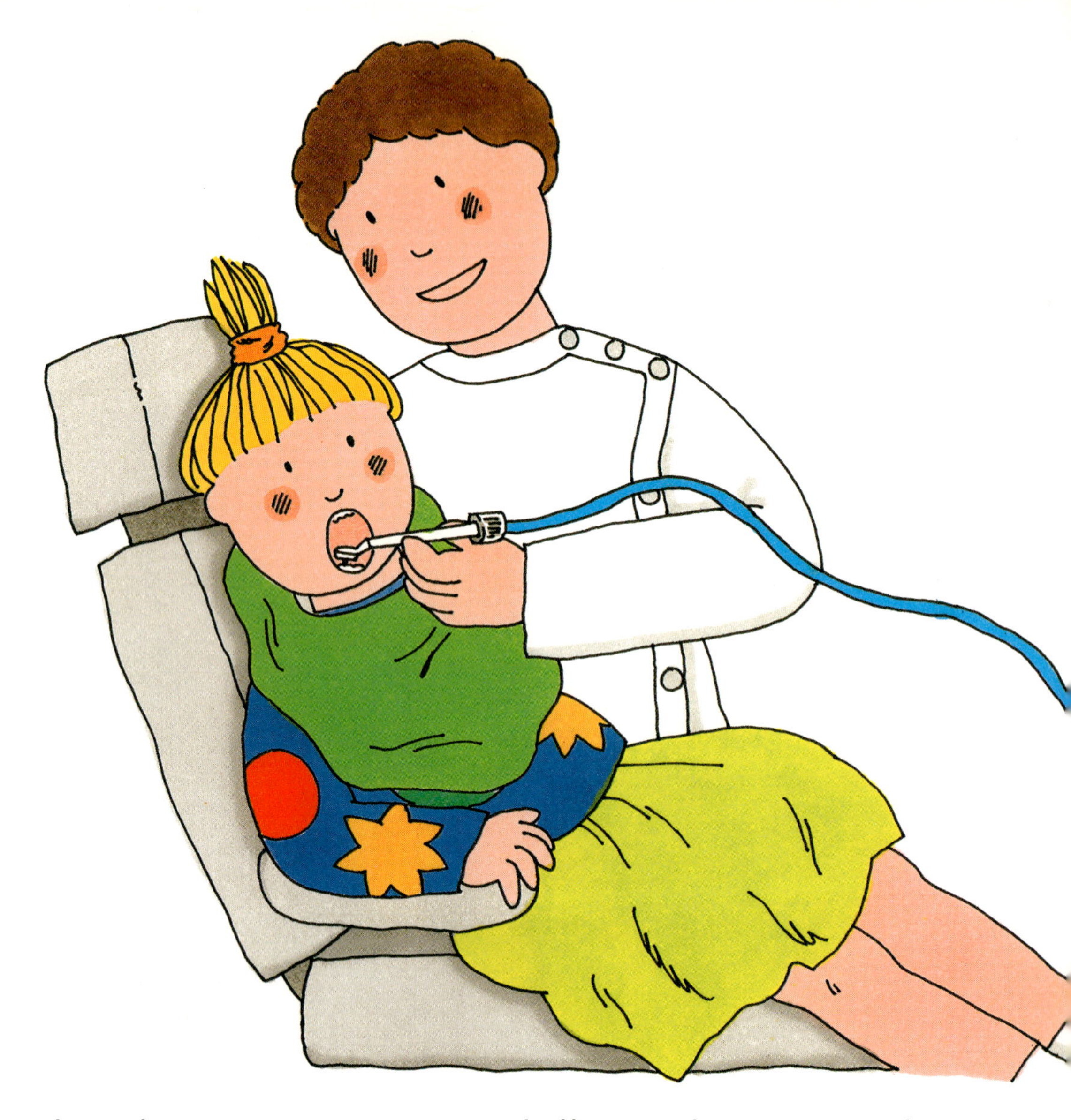

Now the dentist uses a tiny drill to take away the bad part of Sue's tooth. While the drill is inside Sue's mouth, it sounds quite loud.

Mr Watkins tells Sue, 'This is the special mixture that will fill the little hole in your tooth.' It squeaks as the dentist pushes it into the tooth.

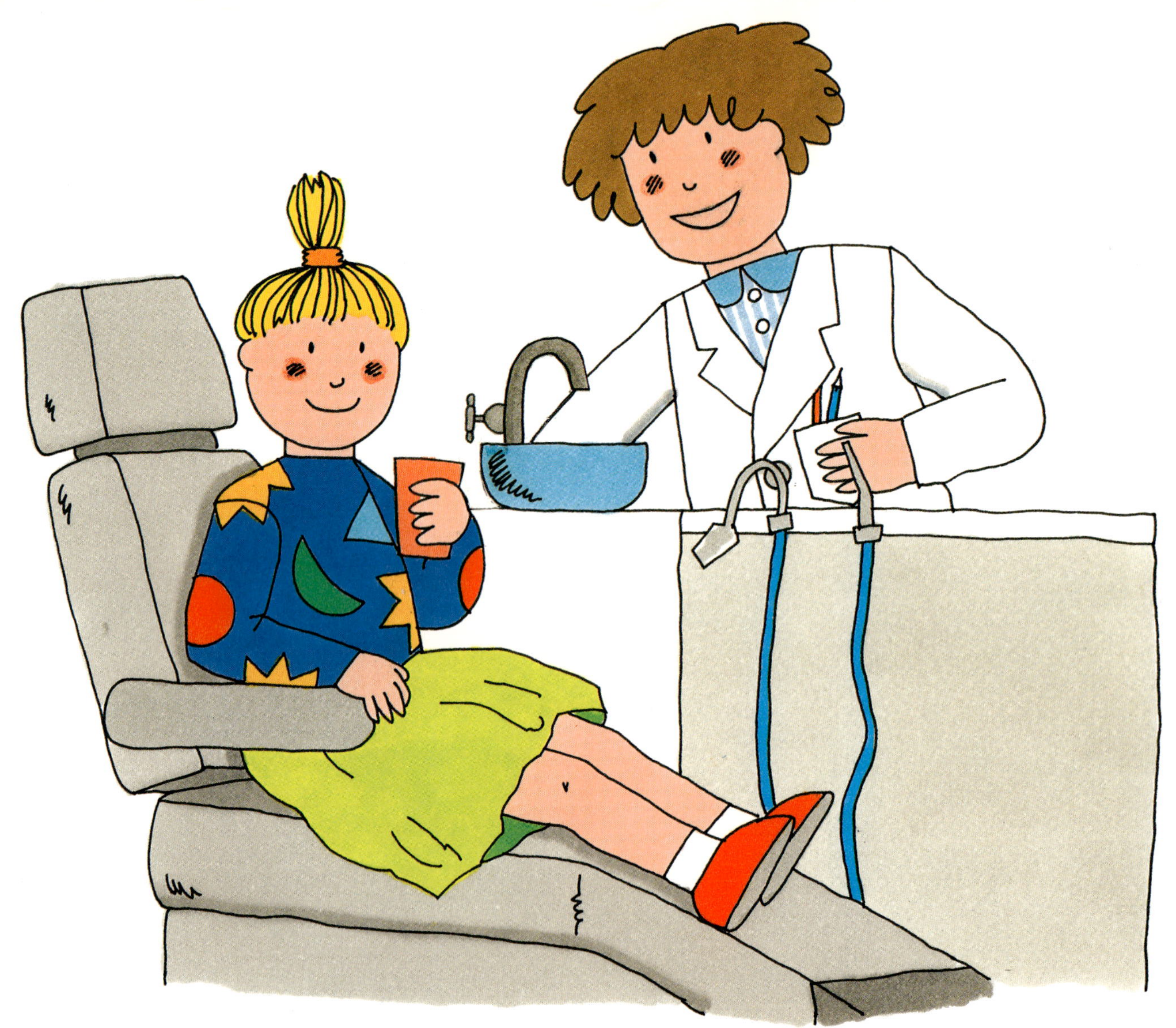

After Mr Watkins has filled Sue's tooth, the nurse gives Sue a glass of special water to rinse the bits out of her mouth.

Mr Watkins shows Sue pictures of the kinds of sugary foods that can make teeth go bad.

'These are better for you and your teeth,' says Mr Watkins. 'But you must brush your teeth after breakfast and before you go to bed.'

Back in the waiting room, Sue sees another boy from school. 'Don't worry,' she tells him. 'It only hurts a little bit!'

Now Sue brushes her teeth every day. 'If I keep my teeth nice and clean,' she says, 'I won't need any fillings when I visit the dentist again.'